Interiors
Collaboration +
Technology

STUDIOS architecture

Introduction by Lisa Findley

Published in Australia in 2009 by

The Images Publishing Group Pty Ltd

ABN 89 059 734 431

6 Bastow Place, Mulgrave, Victoria 3170, Australia

Tel: +61 3 9561 5544 Fax: +61 3 9561 4860

books@imagespublishing.com

www.imagespublishing.com

National Library of Australia Cataloguing-in-Publication entry:

Title: Interiors : collaboration + technology : STUDIOS architecture.

ISBN: 978 1 86470 328 3 (pbk.)

Subjects: STUDIOS architecture.

                   Interior architecture—United States.

                   Architecture and technology—United States.

                   Architecture, American.

Dewey Number: 729.0973

Design development by Default, Anisa Suthayalia and Alex Lin

Production by The Graphic Image Studio Pty Ltd, Mulgrave, Australia
www.tgis.com.au

Pre-publishing services by Splitting Image Colour Studio Pty Ltd, Australia

Printed by Everbest Printing Co. Ltd., in Hong Kong/China

Contents

Imagination, Innovation, Investigation: STUDIOS architecture

Lisa Findley

In the fabric of our collective consciousness, a studio is the territory of an artist. It is an almost mythic space of creativity, of active exploration at the boundaries of imagination, of the struggle against mediocrity. It is also a place of intellectual freedom and active experimentation where success may take many forms and requires perseverance. In a studio, action is taken; something new is made. All of these factors set the idea of a studio apart from the idea of an office. The studio is the office's far more experimental and less rule-bound sibling.

These thoughts were surely in the minds of a group of founding partners when, in 1985, they dubbed their new architectural practice STUDIOS. Rather than use their last names, as is typical in many design firms, the five founders chose an inclusive moniker that embodied their intentions for a non-hierarchical, loosely organized, and generously expansive and collaborative practice. The name also signaled something less overt and more revolutionary: the idea of independent thinking and the urge to redefine the parameters of any project. The name seems to say: This will not be a practice that is content just solving design problems. Instead, this practice will challenge assumptions, investigate cutting-edge technologies, and address evolving cultural and architectural change. And so it has. STUDIOS understands architecture as a cultural practice involved in creating the physical reality of shifting and emerging ways of life.

STUDIOS first made its mark in the late 1980s when it burst onto the scene with bold, experimental designs for the offices of early high-tech companies. These projects quickly demonstrated that STUDIOS was up to the task of discovering form and space for the rapidly evolving workplace culture that was emerging out of the digital revolution. This positioned the practice to ride the crest of the technology wave, moving from quick, cool interior build-outs for techhead bad boys to designing entire campuses for emerging digital giants such as Silicon Graphics and 3Com.

STUDIOS' work now spans a wide range of project types, including civic, institutional, commercial, and industrial projects, while maintaining a deep understanding of the continually evolving world of the contemporary workplace. More than two decades after the firm's founding, the name STUDIOS still reflects the lively, creative, and engaged practice. With partners in Los Angeles, New York, Paris, San Francisco, and Washington, DC, the practice may appear corporate in terms of size and finances, but it remains dedicated to the studio-based exploratory mode of practice that led to its early high-tech successes. This mode is characterized by curiosity, pushing the envelope of expectations, and redefining perceived problems. It is this approach to design, rather than a particular visual style, that constitutes a kind of ethic for STUDIOS and unifies its work across the globe.

As the practice has grown and evolved over time and its project portfolio has expanded, each of its offices has developed depth and expertise in particular kinds of work. At this point in time STUDIOS has two clear bodies of work: architecture and interiors.

STUDIOS provides interior architecture services for the majority of its new construction projects as well as for fit-outs of other new and existing buildings. While this portion of the firm's work grew out of its high-tech days, it continues to evolve through constant innovation and remains always fresh and distinctive. STUDIOS engages in adding value to businesses through design, in breaking new ground through explorations of the workplace by challenging assumptions and redefining perceived problems, in taking on projects for entirely new industries and work practices, and in working in energetic and creative collaboration with a broad range of experts and consultants.

Above La Redoute, Roubaix, France
Previous page Bloomberg LP, New York, NY

STUDIOS continues to help its clients understand the value that good design adds to organizations. A unique, humane, and memorable interior draws business and attracts investors. From an organizational viewpoint, it raises productivity and morale, which in turn increases employee retention and aids recruitment. In an era of intense competition, this may be the edge a business needs to pull ahead of the pack.

One of the clearest indications of STUDIOS' success in adding value to businesses through design is its large number of repeat clients. For instance, the practice has completed multiple projects for Apple Computer, Heller Ehrman LLP, Patchi, Gucci, Bloomberg LP, and the online bank E*Trade.

The Virginia office of E*Trade is a vivid example of the efficient and inventive ways that STUDIOS finds to add value through design. Here STUDIOS drew on its past experience to re-imagine the space as a kind of vertical campus. Two important hallmarks of a campus (academic or otherwise) are lively public spaces that allow for casual social interaction, and a legible structure to the environment. With a single gesture, STUDIOS provides for both of these hallmarks through the introduction of an eight-story atrium threaded with a switchback stair, creating a visual and physical connection between floors. The atrium also floods the center of each floor with daylight and provides a reference point for movement throughout the offices. The large oval stair landings allow employees to stop for a chat without blocking the stairway.

STUDIOS loves to be challenged by complex projects where a wide range of factors and perspectives must be considered and integrated. The firm looks for projects where its abilities as creative and integrative problem-solvers can be fully utilized or, even better, put to the test. Such opportunities are often found before programming for a space has even begun. The strategic planning and pre-design phases are STUDIOS' favorite places to start. Strategic planning can take place without a project site and is a distinctly different exercise from programming: It is not about space and occupancy, but rather how the clients' work activities might be re-imagined.

Through this process, STUDIOS has sometimes ended up rejecting the common approach of matching the design of a space to the apparent outward "culture" of the client. For instance, the first impulse for many designers would have been to make MTV's Times Square location as lively and densely active as the visual culture of the industry. However, in this project STUDIOS took the opposite tack: It created a visually calm environment through the use of subdued color schemes, indirect lighting, and unadorned surfaces. Details are clean and minimal. As a result, the vitality of MTV is present through the programming displayed on the television screens and the movement of the employees within the space.

Similarly, the sleek design and almost residential scale of the New York fitness club Clay counters the expectation that the visual quality of a workout space should match the frenetic pace of a high impact aerobics class. Here, again, it is the human activity, featured against the calm backdrop of the mostly white space, that provides the visual action. The club is a retreat from the chaos of the Manhattan streets outside, a peaceful environment of elegant simplicity in which to focus on the body.

As these projects demonstrate, STUDIOS explores the unique and driving issues for each new commission, re-imagines their visual meaning, and then makes sure that these issues are brought forward all the way through construction. In this way the ideas are seamlessly integrated into the designs, rather than forced or added on to conventional solutions. What emerges are fresh designs specifically tailored to the client, their specific needs, and the possibilities of each space.

STUDIOS believes that the programming phase of a project is not only about planning a space, but also about considering the future of the client business in terms of culture, technology, and branding. Designers must anticipate that a corporation will change over time and that businesses often reorganize, consolidate, or divide their work vertically instead of horizontally or vice-versa.

During programming, STUDIOS explores the functional needs of not only the client business but also of the human beings who are using the space. The work these individuals perform; the way they need to interact with the physical space, technology, and each other; and the relationship of their individual work to that of the larger business are all key considerations.

This ability to look closely at the underlying culture of a business, then to give fresh form to the spaces that it will occupy, is particularly important for what might be termed "category starter" businesses—the first of their kind in a particular field. In these cases, there are no benchmarks about what kind of corporate culture will emerge, how people will want or need to interact in the space, or how the character of the space can contribute to a brand.

XM Satellite Radio is just such a "category starter." The owners of this pioneering satellite radio station were literally inventing the industry when they hired STUDIOS to design their corporate headquarters and broadcast and recording facility, all under the huge roof of a Washington, D.C., warehouse. STUDIOS was challenged to design for a new cutting-edge business with an expected future occupation of 450 employees, based upon the behavior, interaction, and input of an existing group of 44 individuals. From the beginning, XM understood that the space would set the bar for the satellite radio industry. The company recognized that it needed to be a marketing tool, attracting investors and, more critically to the long-term success of the venture, the creative talent of DJs who would leave established local markets for the less secure nation-wide market promised by satellite delivery.

At XM, STUDIOS turned the typical radio station layout on its head. One of the most important places in a traditional radio station is the "jock lounge"—the break room where DJs go to relax and have coffee. At XM, where 120 prefabricated radio booths line the interior of the immense warehouse, the space in between has become the place of escape, the "lounge." In addition, rather than hiding technical requirements in walls, STUDIOS turned them into design elements: Cabling, acoustic panels, and soundproofing all work together to create the aesthetic for the vast space, and allow for easy reconfiguration for the inevitable, yet unpredictable, future function-shifts.

Another way to define an industry through interior design is to re-imagine the spaces occupied by an established industry leader, as STUDIOS did for Bloomberg LP in its New York City office. The office of Cesar Pelli designed the building's core and shell; STUDIOS designed the interior of the Bloomberg Headquarters. The November 2005 cover of *Metropolis* magazine declares "...Bloomberg's dazzling new headquarters transforms our ideas of work, technology, and branding."

Bloomberg was the ideal client for STUDIOS. The corporation views its offices worldwide as a major part of its "brand" and therefore invests heavily in them. In addition, these chic, lively offices are intended to attract and retain the best talent, helping Bloomberg to maintain its position as the lead financial information company in the world.

STUDIOS approached the Bloomberg project as a vertical campus distributed between two mid-rise portions of the building. Generous public spaces and circulation at floors four, five, and six bridge the two sides of the project and become a kind of town center promoting community among the 3,500 people working daily within the security barriers. On the sixth floor, STUDIOS created a huge, sleekly detailed atrium that includes large trees, a rich color palette, stairs and escalators, electronic market zippers, extensive "public" art, and an open market-like kitchen that provides a wide range of selections for full meals or quick snacks. Just off this day-lit atrium are the elegant broadcasting studios, the public face of Bloomberg that is beamed all over the world.

Unlike many office designs, the energy at Bloomberg does not stop at the entry spaces: glassy conference rooms and jewel-like aquaria dot the less public circulation stairs. STUDIOS also designed a flexible desk system that uses sliding barriers to define individual work areas on long shared tables. Managers' work areas are scattered throughout the open offices, encouraging a more collaborative work environment. This not only spatially embodies the flatter organizational structure of Bloomberg; it also effectively provides everyone with a window office.

In the introduction to the 1999 monograph on the work of STUDIOS Architecture, architectural journalist Jim Russell predicted that STUDIOS, based on its pioneering design work in Silicon Valley, would continue to lead the way in re-imagining the workplace. Russell's prediction has come true. Projects like Bloomberg, XM Radio, E*Trade, and the others contained in this volume demonstrate how STUDIOS has become a major global force in interior design. While it is now a powerhouse firm with wide-ranging experience and extensive resources, it maintains all the lively experimental engagement and exploratory curiosity that its name evokes. After the meetings are over, at the end of the day, the designers at STUDIOS are back in the studio.

Bloomberg LP: Headquarters

New York, NY

Services	Interiors
Size	700,000sf/ 65,000m²
Completed	2004–2006

Bloomberg hired STUDIOS to design its new headquarters at 731 Lexington Avenue—a mixed-use building designed by Cesar Pelli and Associates—which features 100,000 square feet of radio and broadcast space, as well as 18 floors of office, conference, and public areas. A sleek atrium on the sixth floor, the "Link," serves as the single point of entry and provides a social hub where employees and visitors can grab a free snack from the pantry or check their email in the communal terminals.

STUDIOS' design concept embodies Bloomberg's organizational mandate for transparency. Open-plan work areas feature adaptable modular workstations and provide window access to all employees. Ninety glass-walled conference rooms in every color of the rainbow are dispersed throughout the space, complementing Bloomberg's signature aquaria and glass-sided koi pond.

Large-scale art and graphic pieces create visual drama in public areas. A vibrant color palette and 100-foot fluorescent light art piece lightens the windowless Training Center.

<u>Left</u> Morse Code-blinking chandelier by artist Cerith Wyn Evans.
<u>Right</u> New York, one of many meeting rooms.

Clockwise from top left Ground-floor lobby security desk.
View of lobby with 88-foot-long cedar installation, *Berwici Pici Pa*,
by artist Ursula von Rydingsvard. Recessed glass koi pond aside
a stairwell in the sixth-floor reception area.

<u>Above</u> *Cloud*, a two-story titanium sculpture by artist
Indigo Manglano-Ovalle.

<u>Clockwise from top</u> Largest of six digital television studios.
One of three full-function radio studios. Spiral escalator leading
to the broadcast center.

<u>Opposite, clockwise from top left</u> View into an open office area. One of 90 glass-enclosed meeting rooms. Typical open-plan workspace.

<u>Clockwise from top left</u> Lounge seating in enclosed meeting room. Seventh-floor auditorium seats up to 300 people. London, one of many meeting rooms. Artist Spencer Finch's *Sunshine* along the aluminum-paneled wall in the training center.

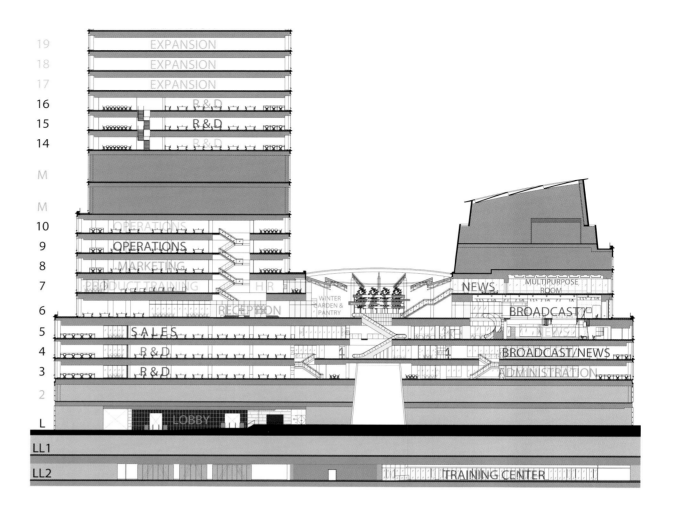

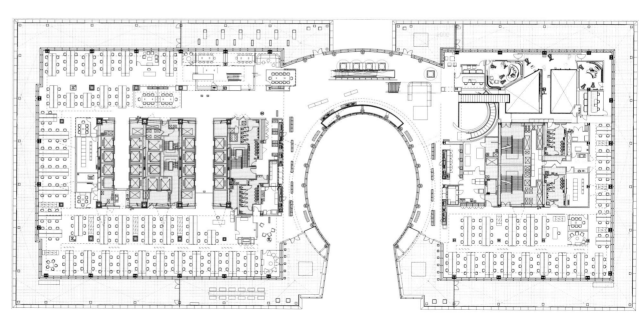

Section diagram showing the arrangement of major
departments and circulation paths.
Bottom Sixth-floor plan.

<u>Clockwise from top left</u> Exterior view of the Link at dusk.
Banded LED display scrolls current news and information.
Close-up of the LED display.

Bloomberg LP: Regional Headquarters

Paris, France

Services	Interiors
Size	60,000sf/ 5,600m²
Completed	2002

Bloomberg asked STUDIOS to design the new home of the firm's operations in France, located within a six-story historic building in the heart of Paris. The first floor houses the more public spaces: TV studios and production spaces, the control room, an auditorium, and the main reception area and cafeteria. All other floors feature open-plan workspaces and glass-walled meeting rooms.

STUDIOS developed a suspended lighting system and a floating acoustic wall that allows for modern technology without compromising the charm of the original ceiling moldings and historic windows. Full-height fish tanks foster a peaceful atmosphere within the hectic environment of international finance. Two granite and steel staircases optimize vertical circulation and form a dramatic connection between floors.

Multimedia is a unifying element on all floors. Television screens feature Bloomberg TV, holographic projections appear on glass walls, ticker tape screens emerge from the pebbled courtyard, and LCD screens are embedded in floors and tables.

Clockwise from left Road access to internal courtyard.
Breakout area. Lobby and main reception.

<u>Above</u> Guest waiting area.

Bloomberg LP: Regional News Bureau

Los Angeles, CA

Services	Interiors
Size	7,500sf/ 700m²
Completed	2002

Bloomberg's Los Angeles Regional News Bureau looks out on the downtown skyline, the iconic Capitol Records building, and the world-famous Hollywood sign. Obstructing window access with hardwall office partitions was never an option. STUDIOS' design for the space—open-plan work areas, simple graphic elements, and glass-walled conference, training, and media rooms—embraces Bloomberg's culture of organizational transparency while showcasing the spectacular city views.

The bureau also includes an "on-air" media room for Bloomberg Financial News, multimedia and teleconference rooms, and a training area. Raised floor mechanical and electrical systems allow a high level of flexibility to accommodate the information services, news, and media company's ever-growing technology and data requirements.

The sleek, open style of the new regional bureau, along with its ubiquitous television and computer monitors, and large signature Bloomberg aquarium, allies with the company's firmwide technology and design themes.

Clay

New York, NY

Services	Interiors
Size	20,000sf/ 1,900m²
Completed	2002

The owners of Clay wanted to create a new kind of fitness center—one that focused on service and design, and emphasized members' comfort in a trainer-friendly environment. Clay is located in the evolving Union Square area of Manhattan, on the second floor of a 1930s building that once housed a furniture showroom. To attract a select clientele seeking the highest standards in a fitness facility, STUDIOS produced a design with a fresh palette and refined materials for Clay's sophisticated downtown members. The space is visually simple and elegant: technological requirements, lighting, and mechanical systems are concealed from view. A fireplace lounge near the entry, a secluded unisex lounge by the locker area, and a rooftop deck provide varied spaces for clients to relax between workouts. Upscale design and a high level of attention to member services mark Clay as the premier facility of its kind in the competitive world of fitness training and health.

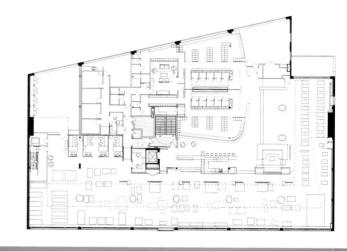

<u>Clockwise from top left</u> Locker room. Floor plan.
Administrative offices. Member lounge.

<u>Above</u> Central seating area.

Entertainment Company

Brussels, Belgium

Services	Interiors
Size	16,200sf/ 1,500m²
Completed	2004

Following a successful collaboration in France, this world-renowned entertainment company asked STUDIOS to develop the design concept for its Belgium office. The project involved the unification of two business groups—a total of 85 staff members—within the recently renovated Tour & Taxi's Entrepot Royal building. The 100-year-old building was selected for its historic character and for the flexibility offered by its large, loft-style floor plates.

STUDIOS' design maintains the company's separate business divisions within a single space, while creating common areas to reunite them. The "community center" and shared services such as coffee and copy points, meeting rooms, and an informal lounge area, are dispersed throughout the space, reinforcing interactivity and communication. Sophisticated lighting and transparent partitions alleviate the relatively dark spaces created by the deep floor plates. Bright color schemes similar to those in the French headquarters were chosen—large orange armchairs and red and orange walls create a cozy atmosphere in the reception area.

<u>Clockwise from top</u> View of open workspace from meeting room.
Detail of community center. Cellular offices.

<u>Above</u> View from atrium walkway.

Entertainment Company

Marne-la-Vallée, France

Services	Interiors
Size	99,000sf/ 9,200m^2
Completed	2003

STUDIOS was selected as the design and programming consultant for the relocation and consolidation of an international entertainment company's French headquarters. During the programming phase, STUDIOS interviewed top management and compiled a client brief and space plan documentation that served as the project's foundation. A "kit of parts" was developed so that STUDIOS could design and validate the building blocks of the project at a very early stage, including typical office, meeting, and support space configurations.

The design reflects the company's corporate image and standards while meeting budgetary objectives and respecting the local culture. Light boxes, soft seating, and curvilinear forms in communal spaces and interstitial areas between the different business divisions encourage interaction between neighbors. Yellow, orange, and red highlights complement neutral grays and natural wood finishes to create individual color schemes on each floor. Flat-panel TVs, display cases, and picture rails showcase the company's diverse video, publishing, and consumer products.

Top Fifty-person screening room.
Bottom Boardroom.
Opposite Double-height reception area.

E*Trade Bank

Arlington, VA

Services	Interiors
Size	120,000sf/ 11,000m²
Completed	2001

STUDIOS created an energized campus-like atmosphere for E*Trade Bank, a division of E*Trade Financial, in a vertical occupancy that reinforces the dynamic nature of the company's workforce. The space was designed in an open-plan concept with no private offices. Workstations are positioned along the building's windowed perimeter, providing staff access to natural light and views. The main corridor circles the support core of the building and is articulated by both an exposed overhead "tray" carrying all data and phone cabling, and by the colorful wood wall, which serves as a unifying and wayfinding feature.

A 600-square-foot, six-story slab opening houses the suspended steel stair, which plays a vital role in unifying all floors in the facility. Each of the five elliptical stair landings features a different artistic floor design expressing E*Trade's flow and connectivity. The stair and atrium top out at the lunchroom, a double-height public space serving as the main employee gathering area.

Top View from conference room of main reception area.
Bottom Top-floor lunchroom and mezzanine.
Opposite View of atrium and suspended interconnecting stair.

LVMH

Paris, France

Services	Interiors, Branding
Size	13,000sf/ 1,200m²
Completed	2003

LVMH-Moët Hennessy Louis Vuitton, the French leader of the world luxury goods market, wanted to foster the reorganization of its product lines through the design of its new Paris headquarters. STUDIOS worked closely with the company to create distinct visual identities for its three emerging branches—Wines & Spirits, Perfumes & Cosmetics, and Watches & Jewelry—while maintaining a cohesive design within the overall context of the building.

The focal point of the space, a glazed double wall vitrine, offers alternating diffuse and direct views of the products displayed within. A detailed oak wall, opposite, is randomly penetrated with niches and highlighted by an integrated lighting system to showcase small iconic objects. STUDIOS collaborated with LVMH's branch presidents and managers to develop a design concept that tells a unique story about each brand. The new space expresses the dualities of the company's culture—innovation and tradition, craftsmanship and industrialization, creativity and organization.

<u>Clockwise from top</u> Product niche wall: Perfumes & Cosmetics.
Large meeting room. Reception desk.
<u>Opposite</u> The Cognac Bar: Wines & Spirits.

La Redoute

Roubaix, France

Services	Interiors
Size	625,000sf/ 58,000m²
Completed	2003–2005

La Redoute, a leader in catalog and online sales of fashion and housewares in Europe, asked STUDIOS to restructure its headquarters, located in a group of industrial buildings. The objective of the project was to improve communication within the company by reorganizing the space around the strategic markets and marketing divisions, and to implement a modern, flexible, and evolving design that would correspond to La Redoute's corporate image.

The new central atrium encourages social interaction among employees and brings new life to the space. Meeting rooms—enclosed by transparent color panels—are dispersed along an interior "boulevard" that links the different buildings. On either side of the boulevard, workstations capitalize on natural light and high ceilings. A bright color palette of orange, yellow, green, pink, and blue was used to define the different floors.

This phased project was successfully implemented over three years in an occupied site and on a very limited budget.

From top Typical floor plan. Cluster of meeting rooms along the "boulevard." Meeting room.
Opposite View through main atrium.

Levi Strauss & Co.

New York, NY

Services	Interiors
Size	40,000sf/ 3,700m²
Completed	2002

STUDIOS designed Levi Strauss & Co.'s new showroom and marketing offices—located in the heart of New York City's Garment District—to support the evolution of the company's time-tested brands. The new space provides a variety of selling environments to suit the showroom's diverse visitor base, and improves the quality of the work environment for the sales staff.

The showroom features an open plan with flexible fixtures and neutral modern fittings that can be configured to accommodate a range of meetings, from an intimate display of garments to a 75-person product presentation or runway fashion show. A multimedia display at the entryway presents promotional information such as market figures and sales events. A "walking tour" overview of the space and its individual exhibit areas provides focused displays for Levi Strauss & Co.'s different brands, including Dockers and Levi's. Guest amenities such as concierge services, catering, seating areas, and workspaces encourage visitors to linger within the showroom.

<u>Above</u> Central seating display area.

<u>Above</u> View of typical showroom from multipurpose room.

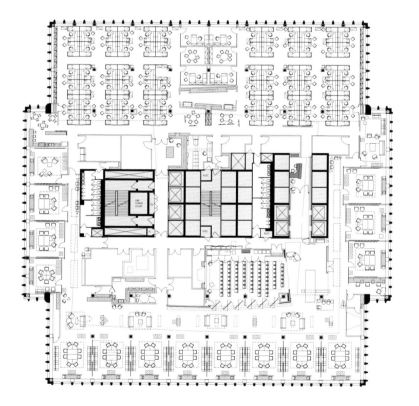

Clockwise from left Detail of architectural feature wall.
Architectural feature wall with panels in open position.
Showroom floor plan.
Opposite Presence and publicity lounge.

Morgan Lewis

Washington, DC

Services	Architecture, Interiors
Size	335,000 sf/ 31,000 m²
Completed	2001

Morgan Lewis, one of Washington, DC's largest law firms, asked STUDIOS to help relocate its offices to a prominent site on Pennsylvania Avenue. The move was necessary to accommodate the firm's growth and to better reflect its position in the legal community.

Extensive renovation to the existing building was required, including the addition of two floors and a new wing featuring a 13-story atrium. STUDIOS collaborated with Carpenter Norris to develop a glass, steel, and Lycra solar light pipe that disperses sunlight—reflected downward from a rooftop mirror—throughout the entire atrium.

The ground floor houses security functions, while public spaces such as the primary reception area, the visitors' business center, and conference rooms reside on the second floor. The thirteenth floor features an employee dining room with a terrace that overlooks the Old Post Office, with views of the Washington Monument and the Capitol.

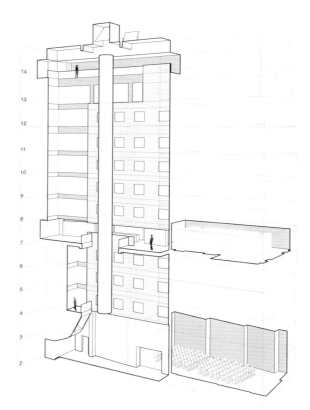

<u>Clockwise from left</u> View of atrium and solar light pipe from the library.
Rooftop heliostat. Atrium and solar light pipe.
<u>Opposite</u> Solar light pipe terminus at second-floor atrium.

MTV Networks

New York, NY

Services   Interiors
Size   28,550sf/ 2,700m²
Completed   2002

MTV Networks retained STUDIOS to design and implement a portion of its New York City headquarters at Times Square. As the new home for the affiliated sales and marketing department, the space makes careful use of light, color, and image to create a dynamic, brand-oriented environment that showcases the wide array of MTV Networks channels and collateral materials created by this group.

The lobby—flanked on either side by dramatic backlit images of large ice chunks aside a lake—offers a rare glimpse of nature in the heart of the urban environment. Individual workplaces and conference rooms, including a flexible lounge and meeting area, are situated around the perimeter of the building. Generous interior corridors throughout the space—accented by glowing acrylic ceilings, light coves, and ephemerally lit plastic mesh—house the pantry, audio/visual area, and magazine library, encouraging interaction among employees.

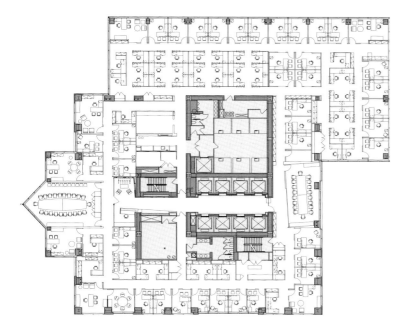

From top Eleventh-floor plan. Conference room.
Opposite View along elevator lobby and reception area.

Orrick, Herrington & Sutcliffe LLP

San Francisco, CA

Services	Strategic Consulting, Interiors
Size	164,000sf/ 15,000m²
Completed	2004

Orrick, Herrington & Sutcliffe selected the top four floors of STUDIOS' Foundry Square 2—an innovative and visionary office development—for its new San Francisco location. The 150-year-old law firm asked STUDIOS to design a state-of-the-art office to meet the needs of its operations, as well as to update its corporate identity.

STUDIOS' design concept accentuates many virtues of the building's core and shell, such as its undulating roofline, the use of canted volumes juxtaposed with more conventional rectilinear forms, and, most important, its transparent glass skin, which provides panoramic views of downtown and floods interior spaces with natural light. Striated and gridded patterns are repeated throughout the project in windows, floor planes, and ceilings. The design creates a modern interpretation of materials typically associated with institutional architecture—wood paneling and stone balance and enrich the office's light-filled interiors. The resulting architecture associates Orrick, Herrington & Sutcliffe with enlightenment and vision.

<u>Above</u> Reception area and conference room.

Above Connecting stair between conference center and law library.

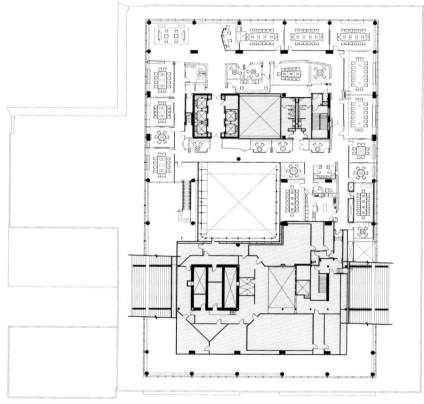

<u>Clockwise from top left</u> Conference room. View from conference room.
View at the building's central light court. Conference center floor plan.

<u>Above</u> Eighth-floor roof deck.

<u>**Orrick, Herrington & Sutcliffe LLP**</u> **STUDIOS architecture**

Patchi

Beirut, Lebanon

Services	Interiors
Size	25,000sf/ 2,300m²
Completed	2004

Patchi asked STUDIOS to develop the design concept for its five-story flagship store in the heart of downtown Beirut. Each floor showcases different Patchi product lines: gourmet chocolates, designer tableware, gifts, cutlery, furnishings, and decorative items.

The ground floor—its large volumes, geometric shapes, and veneering reminiscent of the 1930s—houses the company's most famous product, chocolates. Long, silver-plated counters and a chocolate cave display samples of each type of candy available. The second floor's contemporary design is accentuated by dichotomies in colors and materials: white crystal resin flooring contrasts with ebony, aluminum, and glass furnishings. The third floor is modern and minimalist, with rounded, colorful display tables featuring a variety of gift items. A large helicoidal staircase leads to the fourth and fifth floors. Here, a multicultural "apartment" displays Patchi's eclectic furnishings and decorative items in a harmonious fashion. Tamaris, a dessert restaurant, occupies the walnut-paneled and brushed stainless-steel top floor.

<u>Clockwise from top</u> Ground-floor confectionary area. Tableware display.
Corian wall and gift display.
<u>Opposite</u> Chocolate cave and display.

The Pentagon: Wedges 2–5 Renovation

Arlington, VA

Services	Strategic Consulting, Interiors
Size	5.2 million sf/ 485,000m²
Completed	Wedge 2: 2003, Wedge 3: 2006, Wedge 4: 2008, Wedge 5: 2009

STUDIOS was part of the design/build team chosen to renovate four of the five wedges of The Pentagon. The resulting concept incorporates innovative planning methodology and design while remaining sensitive to the unique characteristics of this historic building. The approach allows The Pentagon to completely redesign its space every four years with each change of the Joint Chiefs of Staff, and supports the frequent modifications required by individual tenants or agencies.

Each wedge of The Pentagon houses 600 user groups with constantly changing facility needs. STUDIOS' flexible space design—along with a hybrid system of adaptable furnishings—allows for 90 percent build-out prior to tenant planning. Work environments can shift from enclosed offices to open-plan without affecting utility distribution or requiring construction.

STUDIOS' concept provides The Pentagon with unlimited planning capabilities, maximum user control and spatial efficiency, and minimizes future costs for necessary modifications over the next 50 years.

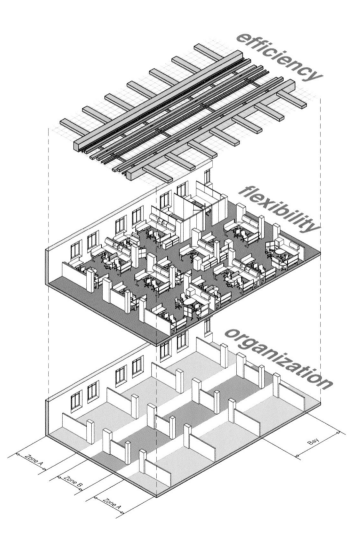

Above Axonometric of planning infrastructure.
Opposite Aerial view of The Pentagon.

Sephora

Boulogne, France

Services   Interiors, Branding
Size   27,000sf/ 2,500m²
Completed   2003

Sephora, a global leader in fragrance and cosmetics, asked STUDIOS to design its new headquarters in a renovated building just outside of Paris. The resulting space reflects the company's youthful and energetic culture while taking cues from the various branding symbols used in the Sephora chain of retail stores.

STUDIOS developed innovative concepts to adapt the existing space for office use. Suspended acoustical ceiling panels in Sephora red bring a more intimate scale to work areas while allowing occupants to appreciate the volume of the space. STUDIOS also designed a partitioning system using polycarbonate panels that allow for the transmission of diffused light while maintaining visual privacy within the semi-enclosed offices and meeting rooms.

A large branding wall—punctuated with product niches and backlit through translucent polycarbonate panels that recall the office partition system—lines the corridor between the reception area and management offices. The wall terminates with a sculptural play of black and white display shelves, inspired by the entry design of typical Sephora retail stores.

Above Typical workstations with acoustical treatment.
Opposite Branding and product display.

Stone & Youngberg

San Francisco, CA

Services	Strategic Consulting, Interiors
Size	30,000sf/ 2,800m²
Completed	2003

STUDIOS was chosen by Stone & Youngberg, a growing investment banking firm, to develop its new headquarters in San Francisco's historic Ferry Building. The design emphasizes the theatrical nature of the space by placing most of the company's operations on view. Open-plan trading areas and office zones appear as distinct entities that "float" within the vast space.

The Ferry Building is a National Register landmark, and any new construction must be removable without damaging the original structure. To meet these requirements, STUDIOS created a series of "parabuildings" within the existing structure to house conference rooms and private offices. Wood wall panels, railings, counters, and other elements were incorporated into the design to complement the original stone and steel features, and to bring warmth to the space.

The two-level lobby and conferencing area juxtaposes modern forms with the building's historic fabric and systems. A custom curved ceiling is suspended over the trading floor, improving acoustics and drawing focus to the heart of the company.

<u>Clockwise from top</u> View of one of two break areas.
Reception area. Central trading area.

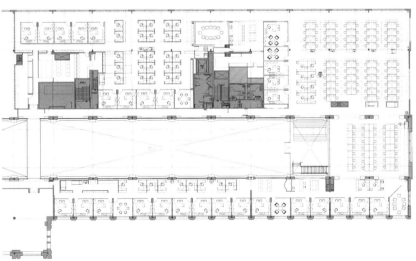

Left Office zone with wood lattice.
Right Floor plan.

Above View of reception area from exterior corridor.
Opposite Conference room.

Venable LLP

Washington, DC

Services	Strategic Consulting, Interiors
Size	243,000sf/ 22,600m²
Completed	2003

Venable asked STUDIOS to develop a design concept for its Washington, DC, office. The 100-year-old law firm wanted an efficient design with a clean, modern aesthetic that would promote stability and professionalism.

The project called for the integration of new construction with the historic renovation of the landmark Hecht Department Store buildings. A series of ramp and stair connections were created to compensate for disparate floorplate alignments between the new and the historic structures, establishing a more cohesive office atmosphere.

Public spaces such as reception and lobby areas share common design elements, including floating Venetian plaster panels that frame enormous stainless-steel pendant lighting fixtures. A ceremonial stair connects a training center to the street-level reception. Attorney practice areas are located on the upper levels. The top floor of the building opens out onto a rooftop terrace with an outdoor dining area and a bocce ball court, encouraging relaxation and social interaction among employees.

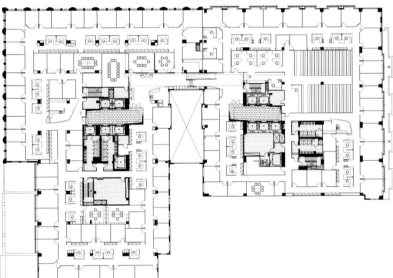

<u>Clockwise from top left</u> Elevator lobby. Large multipurpose room.
Rooftop terrace. Typical attorney practice floor plan.
<u>Opposite</u> Conference center lobby on top floor.

VennWorks

New York, NY

Services	Interiors
Size	25,000sf/ 2,300m²
Completed	2001

VennWorks asked STUDIOS to design a space that reflected its unique business model. The company has two distinct components: the creation of new technologies and the implementation of infrastructure to support these new businesses. STUDIOS developed a design to both reflect and harmonize with this duality.

A bright blue lighting element reflects off the lobby's mirrored ceiling and crosses the linear waiting area, connecting office functions at each end of the floor plate. The reception floor links to a loft-like space beneath a steeply sloped roof from which three new 17-foot skylights provide natural illumination. A stair with translucent blue resin treads, glass rails, and open risers leads up to the main conference rooms, a break area, and an employee lounge. The perimeter offices' etched glass walls provide continuous light and sight lines through the space. Concrete covered steel columns were stripped to reveal their steel bolts and then sealed with fireproof intumescent bright red paint.

<u>Above</u> View of lobby and reception area.

<u>Clockwise from top</u> Workstations and perimeter offices.
Interior workstations with light slot. Sixteenth-floor plan.

XM Satellite Radio: Live Performance Studio

Washington, DC

Services	Interiors
Size	2,000sf/ 185m²
Completed	2000

XM Satellite Radio is a nationwide, digital radio system broadcast via satellite. Located in a 19th-century brick-and-concrete former printing plant, XM's corporate headquarters, with its broadcast and recording facility, contains more than 100 individual studios. XM's numerous technical requirements have been incorporated into the design—exposed data cables and acoustic panels contribute to the overall aesthetic of the space and provide flexibility for future reconfiguration.

The Live Performance Studio is the keystone of the state-of-the-art digital broadcast complex, and is one of the most sophisticated recording facilities in the United States. The entire studio and control room are detached from the building structure by vibration isolators. Sized to accommodate a range of performances—from soloists to small orchestras—the studio was designed to the highest level of acoustic engineering. It also serves as a performance space for visiting artists and can hold audiences of up to 50 people.

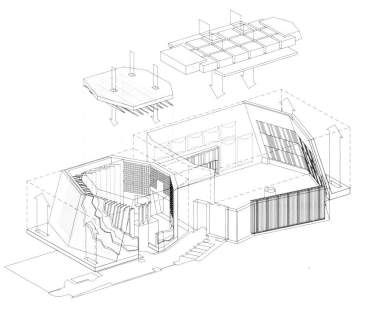

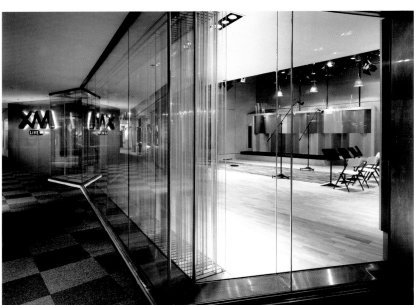

<u>Clockwise from top</u> View of control room, looking out into live room.
Custom glass diffuser wall at live room.
Axonometric diagram of performance studio.
<u>Opposite</u> View from hallway into live room.

Project Credits

Bloomberg LP: Headquarters
New York, NY, 2004–2006

Principal-in-Charge: Todd DeGarmo
Design Team: Tom Krizmanic, Brian Tolman, Mike Krochmaluk, Geoff Deold, Brooke Luckock, Sohith Perera
Structural Engineer: Weidlinger Associates, Inc.
Mechanical Engineer: Cosentini Associates
General Contractor: Structure Tone, Inc.
Project Manager: Turner Construction
Environmental Graphic Design: Pentagram
Art Consultant: The Public Art Fund
IT Consultant: CS Technology
Elevator Consultant: BOCA Group International, Inc.
Code Consultant: Milrose Consultants, Inc.
Acoustical Consultant: Shen Milsom & Wilke
Food Consultant: Cini-Little International, Inc.
Security Consultant: Kroll Schiff & Associates, Inc.
Specialty AV: Scharf Weisberg, Inc.
Broadcast Studio Set Designer: Production Design Group / Jack Morton Worldwide
Broadcast Integrators: Communications Engineering, Inc.
Broadcast Lighting Designers: The Lighting Design Group
Client: Bloomberg LP
Photographer: Eric Laignel, Paul Warchol

Bloomberg LP: Regional Headquarters
Paris, France, 2002

Principal-in-Charge: Pierre Pastellas
Design Team: Sonia Jacobs, Sigi Schultz
Structural Engineer: Terrell Rooke Associates
Code Consultant: APAVE
Health and Security Consultant: GEMO
MEP Engineer: Flack + Kurtz
General Contractor: IASA
Client: Bloomberg LP
Photographer: Philippe Caulliez, Eric Laignel

Bloomberg LP: Regional News Bureau
Los Angeles, CA , 2002

Principal-in-Charge: Christopher Mitchell
Design Team: Sandra Page Mitchell, Mariapaz Trillo, Jeff Wou, Franco Chan
Structural Engineer: John A. Martin & Associates
General Contractor: Swinerton Builders
Lighting: Architecture & Light
Client: Bloomberg LP
Photographer: Tom Bonner

Clay
New York, NY, 2002

Principal-in-Charge: Todd DeGarmo
Design Team: John Henderson, Brent Capron, Stephanie Cheng
Structural Engineer: Severud Associates Consulting Engineers
MEP Engineer: Thomas Veltre Associates
General Contractor: Interior Construction Corp.
Lighting: Thompson + Sears Lighting, LLC
Client: Clay, LLC
Photographer: Eric Laignel, Doug Fogelson

Entertainment Company
Brussels, Belgium, 2004

Principal-in-Charge: Pierre Pastellas
Design Team: Gary Tschirhart, Muriel Zeller
Local Architect: Sicabel
MEP Engineer: Sicabel
General Contractor: Super Build
Acoustic: Scala Consultants
Health and Security Consultant: W4R
Lighting: Philippe Michel
Client: Confidential
Photographer: Luc Boegly

Entertainment Company
Marne-la-Vallée, France, 2003

Principal-in-Charge: Pierre Pastellas
Design Team: Gary Tschirhart, Nicolas Vignot, Sys Bisgaard, David Burns
Restaurant Consultant: Restauration Conseil
MEP Engineer: Barbanel
Project Management: Hanscomb/GEMO
General Contractor: Super Build
Acoustic/Screening Room: Studio Bau:ton (Los Angeles)
Lighting: Aartill
Code Consultant: Qualiconsult
Health and Safety Consultant: Qualiconsult
Client: Confidential
Photographer: Luc Boegly

E*Trade Bank
Arlington, VA, 2001

Principal-in-Charge: Todd DeGarmo
Design Team: Tom Krizmanic, Erik Sueberkrop, Jim Gerrety, Pablo Quintana, Doug Koschalk, Larry Levy
Structural Engineer: Shenberger & Associates, Inc.
MEP Engineer: GHT, Limited
General Contractor: Clark Construction Group, LLC
Lighting: Light'n Up
Client: E*Trade Financial
Photographer: Michael Moran Photography

LVMH
Paris, France, 2003

Principal-in-Charge: James Cowey
Design Team: David Burns, Isabelle Jannin, Charlotte Harang
Mechanical Engineer: SECATH
Electricity Consultant: KEE
Project Management: SETEC
General Contractor: Super Build
Code Consultant: Socotec
Client: LVMH
Photographer: Jean-Christophe Galmiche

La Redoute
Roubaix, France, 2003–2005

Principal-in-Charge: Pierre Pastellas
Design Team: Alexandra Villegas, Stephen Chambers, Charlotte Harang
Project Management: 2ID
Structural Engineer: SODEG
MEP Engineer: SODEG
Code Consultant: Bureau Veritas
Client: La Redoute
Photographer: Luc Boegly

Levi Strauss & Co.
New York, NY, 2002

Principal-in-Charge: Todd DeGarmo
Design Team: Linda Jacobs, Brent Capron
Mechanical Engineer: Syska & Hennessy
General Contractor: Lehr Construction
Client: Levi Strauss & Co.
Photographer: Andrew Bordwin

Morgan Lewis
Washington, DC, 2001

Principal-in-Charge: Todd DeGarmo
Design Team: Jim Gerrety, Tim Kearney, Christian Amolsch, Marnique Heath, Abram Goodrich, David Knudson
Structural Engineer: Simpson, Gumpertz & Heger, Inc.
Mechanical Engineer: Engineers Design Group
General Contractor: HITT Contracting, Inc.
Signage Design: Signs Unlimited
Light Pipe Design: Carpenter Norris Consulting
Lighting: Light'n Up
Foodservice Consultant: Cini-Little International, Inc.
Elevator Consultant: Lerch, Bates & Associates, Inc.
Client: Morgan Lewis LLP
Photographer: Paul Warchol Photography

MTV Networks
New York, NY, 2002

Principal-in-Charge: Todd DeGarmo
Design Team: Tom Krizmanic, Althea Cheng
Mechanical Engineer: Arthur Metzler & Associates
General Contractor: Lehr Construction
Graphic Design: STUDIOS Architecture
Client: MTV Networks
Photographer: Eric Laignel

Orrick, Herrington & Sutcliffe LLP
San Francisco, CA, 2004

Principal-in-Charge: Thomas K. Yee
Design Team: Leif Glomset, Karen Koenig, Aaron Ragan, Sharon Lahr, Chris Kimball, Sarah Beach
Structural Engineer: Nishkian Menninger
MEP Engineer: Alfa Tech Consulting Engineers
General Contractor: Swinerton Builders
Signage Design: Propp + Guerin
Signage Fabrication: Weidner Architectural Signage
Landscape Architect: The SWA Group
A/V: Shen Milsom & Wilke/Paoletti
Telecommunications: Teledata Communications
Lighting: Architecture & Light
Food Service Consultant: The Marshall Associates
Code Consultant: Rolf Jensen and Associates
Client: Orrick, Herrington & Sutcliffe LLP
Photographer: Tim Griffith, Fotoworks/Benny Chan

Patchi
Beirut, Lebanon, 2004

Principal-in-Charge: Pierre Pastellas
Design Team: Jean-Pascal Crouzet, David Burns, Isabelle Jannin
Local Architect: Adel Samarah, Dr Jaizari Office
Structural Engineer: Dr Jaizari Office
MEP Engineer: Dr Jaizari Office
Lighting: Philippe Michel
Client: Patchi
Photographer: Luc Boegly, Maya Kanakry

The Pentagon: Wedges 2–5 Renovation
Arlington, VA, 2003–2009

Principal-in-Charge: Christopher Budd
Design Team: Larry Levy, Matthew Ronan, Jes Smith, Casey Lim, Bill Young, Bianca Branch, Nathan Morris, Esther Springer
Base Building Architect: Shalom Baranes Associates
Structural Engineer: Tadjer-Cohen-Edelson Associates, Inc.
Mechanical Engineer: Southland Industries
Civil/Fire Protection: Schirmer Engineering
General Contractor: Hensel Phelps Construction Co.
A/V: General Dynamics
Electrical/Lighting: M.C. Dean, Inc.
Code Consultant: Ferguson Engineering
Client: Department of Defense

Sephora
Boulogne, France, 2003

Principal-in-Charge: James Cowey
Design Team: Muriel Zeller, Delphine Cunin
MEP Engineer: Flack + Kurtz
Construction Manager: Cabinet FT
Code Consultant: Socotec
Client: Sephora
Photographer: Luc Boegly

Stone & Youngberg
San Francisco, CA, 2003

Principal-in-Charge: Erik Sueberkrop
Design Team: Julia Campbell, Douglas Oleson, Nicholas Tsuk
Structural Engineer: Rutherford and Chekene
MEP Engineer: Glumac
General Contractor: Hathaway Dinwiddie Construction Group
Project Manager and Estimator: The Rockridge Group
Telecommunications: Teledata Communications
Historic: Page & Turnbull, Inc.
Acoustic: Charles Salter Associates
Lighting: Architecture & Light
Client: Stone & Youngberg LLC
Photographer: Tim Griffith

Venable LLP
Washington, DC, 2003

Principal-in-Charge: Todd DeGarmo
Design Team: Jason DeChambeau, Abram Goodrich, Christian Ai Marnique Heath, Brian Pilot
Structural Engineer: Thornton-Tomasetti-Cutts, Inc.
MEP Engineer: Girard Engineering
General Contractor: Clark Construction Group, LLC
Construction Manager: Mark G. Anderson Consultants
Lighting: MCLA
Food Service Consultant: Cini-Little International, Inc.
Client: Venable LLP
Photographer: Paul Warchol Photography

VennWorks
New York, NY, 2001
Principal-in-Charge: Todd DeGarmo
Project Team: Tom Krizmanic, Kevin Estrada, Sean Brown
MEP Engineer: Lilker Associates
General Contractor: Lehr Construction
Client: VennWorks
Photographer: Wayne Sorce

XM Satellite Radio: Live Performance Studio
Washington, DC, 2000

Principal-in-Charge: I. Guyman Martin
Design Team: Ronald Ngiam, William Deegan, Abram Goodrich, Nathan
Minch, Matthew Geiss, Robert Nehrebecky, David Baker, Bryan Chun,
Kristen Breiten, Jes Smith
Structural Engineer: Rathgeber/Goss Associates
MEP Engineer: GHT, Limited
General Contractor: James G. Davis Construction Corp.
Acoustical: Shen Milsom & Wilke, Francis Daniel Consulting Alliance
Lighting: George Sexton Associates
Broadcast: Northeastern Communications, Inc.
Client: XM Satellite Radio
Photographer: Michael Moran Photography,
Hoachlander Davis Photography

Notable Awards

AIA New York,
Interior Architecture,
Merit Award, 2007
Bloomberg LP Headquarters
New York, NY

AIA National Institute,
Honor Award for Interior
Architecture, 2007
Bloomberg LP Headquarters
New York, NY

Society for College and
University Planning (SCUP)/
AIA-CAE Awards, Honor
Award for Restoration,
Renovation or Adaptive
Reuse, 2007
University of California,
Santa Barbara
De La Guerra Dining
Commons
Santa Barbara, CA

Business Week/Architectural
Record Award, 2006
Bloomberg LP Headquarters,
New York, NY

Business Week/Architectural
Record Merit Award, 2006
State of California,
Dept. of Health Services,
Laboratory Campus
Phase III Office Building
Richmond, CA

The Chicago Athenaeum,
American Architecture
Award, 2006
State of California,
Dept. of Health Services,
Laboratory Campus
Phase III Office Building
Richmond, CA

Gold Nugget Merit Award
and Grand Award, 2006
State of California,
Dept. of Health Services,
Laboratory Campus
Phase III Office Building
Richmond, CA

AIA East Bay Awards,
Architecture Merit Award,
2005
State of California,
Dept. of Health Services,
Laboratory Campus
Phase III Office Building
Richmond, CA

AIA San Francisco Design
Awards, Excellence in
Interior Architecture
Citation, 2005
Orrick Herrington
and Sutcliffe, LLP
San Francisco, CA

AIA New York Design
Awards,
Interior Architecture,
Merit Award, 2005
Bloomberg LP Headquarters
New York, NY

AIA Washington, DC,
Award of Excellence in the
Historic Resources Category,
2004
Christ Church of Georgetown
Washington, DC

AIA San Francisco Design
Awards/Best of the Bay,
Excellence in Design Award,
2003
Milpitas City Hall
Milpitas, CA

DuPont Antron Design
Awards, Large Office
Category,
Silver Award, 2003
*E*Trade Bank*
Arlington, VA

IDSA Industrial Design
Excellence Award,
sponsored by Business
Week, Silver Award, 2003
XM Satellite Radio
Washington, DC

AIA Washington, DC,
Interior Design Awards, 2003
Morgan Lewis
Washington, DC

AIA Washington, DC,
Merit Award, 2002
XM Satellite Radio
Washington, DC

AIA California Council,
Firm of the Year Award, 2002
Design Excellence

The Chicago Athenaeum,
American Architecture
Award, 2002
University of Cincinnati
Medical and Pharmacy
School Expansion
Cincinnati, OH

International Interior
Design Association,
Washington
Metropolitan Chapter,
Silver Award, 2002
*E*Trade*
Alpharetta, GA

AIA San Diego, CA,
Interior Design Award, 2002
Industrial and Commercial
Bank of China
Shanghai, China

AIA Santa Clara Valley, CA,
Details Award, 2001
SGI Customer Briefing Center
Mountain View, CA

FX International Interior
Design Awards, Finalist,
Large Office Category, 2001
XM Satellite Radio
Washington, DC

International Interior
Design Association,
Washington
Metropolitan Chapter,
Bronze Award, 2001
XM Satellite Radio
Washington, DC

International Interior
Design Association,
Washington
Metropolitan Chapter,
Gold Award, 2001
The Washington Capitals
Washington, DC

AIA San Mateo, CA,
Merit Award, 2000
Bayview Plaza Renovation
San Mateo, CA

AIA Pittsburgh, PA,
Honor Award, 2000
Marconi Communications
Headquarters
Warrendale, PA

Interiors Magazine,
Environmental Graphic
Design Award, 2000
225 Varick Street
New York, NY

AIA Washington, DC,
Merit Award, 2000
Arthur Andersen
Baltimore, MD

Industrial Designer's
Society of America IDEA
Award, Silver Award, 2000
Arthur Andersen
Baltimore, MD

International Interior
Design Association,
Washington, DC, Chapter,
Gold Award, 2000
Arthur Andersen
Baltimore, MD

International Interior
Design Association,
Washington, DC, Chapter,
Bronze Award, 2000
SAP America Headquarters
Newtown Square, PA

AIA Santa Clara Valley, CA,
Honor Award, 1999
Equipment for Technology
& Science
San Jose, CA

AIA San Francisco, CA,
Honor Award, 1999
STUDIOS Architecture,
San Francisco Office
San Francisco, CA

City of Mountain View
Mayor's Award, 1998
Silicon Graphics, Inc.,
North Charleston Campus
Mountain View, CA

International Interior
Design Association,
Washington Metropolitan
Chapter, Silver Award, 1998
Discovery Channel
Latin America
Miami, FL

Buildings Magazine New
Construction Awards, 1998
Special Spaces Category,
FORE Systems,
53 Bites Café
Warrendale, PA

Gold Nugget,
Award of Merit, 1998
Equipment for
Technology and Science
San Jose, CA

AIA Santa Clara Valley, CA,
Honor Award, 1997
Silicon Graphics, Inc.,
North Charleston Campus
Mountain View, CA

AIA Santa Clara Valley, CA,
Honor Award, 1997
3Com Corporation,
Great America Campus,
Phase II
Santa Clara, CA

Gold Nugget,
Grand Award, 1997
3Com Corporation,
Great America Campus,
Phase II
Santa Clara, CA

AIA San Francisco, CA,
Honor Award, 1996
Silicon Graphics, Inc.,
Silicon Studio
Mountain View, CA

AIA Santa Clara Valley, CA,
Honor Award, 1995
Silicon Graphics, Inc.,
Shoreline Entry Site
Mountain View, CA

AIA California Council,
Merit Award, 1995
Silicon Graphics, Inc.,
Shoreline Entry Site
Mountain View, CA

Interntional Interior
Design Association, 1995
International Trade Mart
Osaka, Japan

Gold Nugget Award, 1995
Silicon Graphics, Inc.,
Shoreline Entry Site
Mountain View, CA

Gold Nugget Award, 1994
Synoptics Communications,
Inc., Manufacturing Facility
Santa Clara, CA

Gold Nugget Award, 1994
University of California,
Davis, Alumni &
Visitors Center
Davis, CA

AIA San Francisco, CA,
Merit Award, Interior, 1994
Knoll Exhibit at Orgatec
Cologne, Germany

AIA National Honor Award,
Interior Architecture, 1993
Knoll International
Showroom
Frankfurt, Germany

AIA California Council
Award, 1993
Apple Computer
European HQ & Training
Center
London, England

AIA California Council
Award, 1993
3Com Corporation,
European HQ &
Manufacturing
Ireland

AIA San Francisco, CA,
Beyond the Bay Awards, 1993
3Com Corporation,
European HQ &
Manufacturing
Ireland

Institute of Business
Designers / Potomac
Chapter Awards, 1993

— Outstanding
Achievement Awards
Milbank, Tweed, Hadley &
McCloy, Law Office
Washington, DC
Varet Marcus & Fink,
Law Office
Washington, DC

— Creative Use of
Architectural Planning
MCI Communications
Corporation, Corporate HQ
Washington, DC

— Creative Use of Lighting
Chevron, USA Government
Affairs Office
Washington, DC

— Creative Use of Color
Varet Marcus & Fink, Law
Office
Washington, DC

— Creative Use of Materials
Milbank, Tweed, Hadley &
McCloy, Law Office
Washington, DC

AIA San Francisco, CA,
Design Excellence, 1993
3Com Corporation
European HQ &
Manufacturing
Ireland

AIA California
Merit Awards, 1993
3Com Corporation
European HQ & Manufacturing
Ireland
Apple Computer Training
& Systems Development
England

Industrial Design
Excellence Awards (IDEA),
sponsored by
Business Week, 1993
ORGATEC Exhibit, Silver
Knoll Group Showroom,
Bronze

City of Mountain View
Mayor's Award, 1992
Silicon Graphics
Computer Systems
Mountain View, CA

AIA San Francisco, CA,
Award of Merit, 1992
The Knoll Group, Retail
Germany

Drywall Institute Design
Award, 1992
Silicon Graphics Inc.,
Building 10
Mountain View, CA

Interiors Magazine, National,
Best Office Interior Award,
1991
Apple Computer
Learning Center
Cupertino, CA

AIA California,
Design Award, 1991
Silicon Graphics, Inc.,
Systems Software Division
Mountain View, CA

Gold Nugget,
Merit Award, 1991
3Com Corporation, Great
America Campus
Santa Clara, CA

International Design
Magazine, Design Award,
1991
"The Art of Architecture,"
Exhibition at LIMN
San Francisco, CA

California State Historic
Preservation Award, 1991
Orrick, Herrington &
Sutcliffe Law Offices
Old Federal Reserve
Bank Building
San Francisco, CA

AIA Santa Clara, CA,
Citations, 1991
Silicon Graphics, Inc.,
World-Class Manufacturing
Mountain View, CA
Silicon Graphics, Inc.,
Systems Software Division
Mountain View, CA

AIA San Francisco, CA,
Design Award, 1990
Silicon Graphics, Inc.,
Advanced Systems Division
Mountain View, CA

AIA Washington, DC,
Merit Award, 1990
Apple Computer,
Regional Sales Office
New York, NY

Mayor's Annual
Environment Design Award,
Washington, DC, 1989
Herman Miller Office Pavilion
Washington, DC

Institute of Business
Designers Potomac Award,
1989
Arnold & Porter,
Lafayette Center
Washington, DC

Drywall Information
Trust Award, 1989
Silicon Graphics, Inc.,
Work Products Division
Mountain View, CA

Washington, DC Design
Celebration Competition

Interiors Magazine and
Washington, DC AIA, 1989
Rogovin, Huge & Schiller
Washington, DC
Herman Miller Office
Pavilion Showroom
Washington, DC
Apple Computer
Government Affairs
Washington, DC

National Institute of
Business Designers/
Interior Design Magazine,
Outstanding Achievement
Award, 1988
3Com Corp., Manufacturing
& Engineering, Building 1
Santa Clara, CA

Architecture Magazine,
National Interior Design
Award, 1987
Apple Computer,
Advanced Computer
Technology Center
Cupertino, CA

AIA San Francisco, CA,
Design Awards, 1987
Apple Computer,
Advanced Computer
Technology Center
Cupertino, CA

Principal Biographies

Christopher Budd

Christopher came to STUDIOS in 1989 and was promoted to principal in 2005. He is currently the managing principal of the Washington, DC office.

Christopher's passion for the human aspect of design led to the creation of STUDIOS' Consulting Services, which employs new methodologies for examining an organization's unique needs and challenges. He created ethnographic research tools to analyze clients' business objectives in order to appropriately align the work environment in terms of identified work processes and measurable outcomes. In addition, Christopher develops innovative interior infrastructures that respond to high levels of user control, cost containment, and changing needs. As a result of this work, he was invited to join the US General Services Administration's Workplace 2020, a government think tank whose mission is to develop a strong approach to analyzing workplace performance.

One of Christopher's most notable projects was the strategic planning, master planning, and space planning of 4,500,000 square feet for the Pentagon. He also led the renovation of the GSA headquarters in DC, as well as strategic planning and design efforts for Accenture's European headquarters in London. Past clients include the Coca-Cola Company, Andersen, Bates USA, and Discovery Channel Latin America.

In 1983, Christopher graduated from the University of Kansas with a Bachelor of Fine Arts with a focus on Systemic Design, and minor concentrations in Art History, Architectural Engineering, and Literature. In 1997, he was awarded a Master of Science in Environmental Analysis and Design from Cornell University, where he focused his research and thesis on digital multimedia as a tool for learning.

James Cowey
AIA, MBA

Jim is currently the managing principal of the Paris office and a member of the firm-wide executive committee. He joined STUDIOS in 1996.

Jim has contributed significantly to the development of the Paris office and has helped to increase the firm's presence in Europe. He has been instrumental in leading that office's diversification to include high technology clients like eBay and Cisco Systems, as well as corporate and retail clients such as The Gap, Sephora, and LVMH Moët Hennessy-Louis Vuitton. Jim is currently working with Frank Gehry Partners on a new museum project in Paris.

Jim holds a Bachelor of Science in Architecture from the University of Virginia and a Master of Architecture from Rice University. He also holds a Master of Business Administration from the HEC School of Management in Paris. He is a member of the Board of Directors of the AIA Continental Europe Chapter.

Todd DeGarmo
FAIA, LEED® AP

Todd came to STUDIOS' Washington, DC office in 1989, and founded the New York office in 1995. He currently serves as CEO and chair of the firm-wide executive committee.

Todd has developed a strong expertise in guiding organizations through the complete design and construction process, including site search, strategic planning, and master planning exercises. In addition, he has considerable experience helping emerging companies envision new work environments that support and integrate their culture, work processes, technology, and brand. Todd's recent projects include the award-winning Bloomberg LP headquarters in New York and E*Trade Bank's headquarters in Virginia, as well as extensive interiors work for Washington, DC law firms Venable and Morgan Lewis.

Past projects include a regional sales office and showroom for NIKE, SAP America's headquarters, and post-9/11 strategic planning and relocation services for New York's Port Authority. Todd was also selected through the General Service Administration's Design Excellence program to participate on the team for the renovation of the historic GSA building at 1800 F Street in Washington, DC.

Todd earned his degree in architecture from the University of Cincinnati in 1980. He is active in the AIA, the Partnership for New York City, and the National Building Museum.

Charles Dilworth
FAIA, LEED® AP

Charles joined STUDIOS in 1988, and became a principal in 1995. He is currently the managing principal of the San Francisco office.

Whether high-tech, civic, or educational, Charles' projects celebrate the optimism of technology and architectural innovation. He views architecture as an instrument to structure social interaction and cognitive awareness, where the cultural heritage of a project—including the natural history of a site—is explored to define its physical properties. As a LEED-accredited professional, he also advocates architecture that embraces the technology and strategies of sustainable design.

Charles is currently serving as principal in charge for the new University of California at Merced Social Sciences and Management Building and the Santa Teresa Branch Library for the City of San Jose. He also recently served as principal in charge/design principal for the Evergreen Branch Library and the new Milpitas City Hall, winner of a 2005 Chicago Athenaeum Award. His work on the Department of Health Services Office Building for the State of California has earned both a 2006 Chicago Athenaeum Award and a 2006 Business Week/ Architectural Record Merit Award. Charles' past projects include the California Teachers' Association headquarters and the 500,000-square-foot Silicon Graphics North Charleston campus.

Charles studied architecture at Yale University, where he received a Bachelor of Arts, cum laude, in 1979 and a Master of Architecture in 1983. He is an Adjunct Professor of Architecture at the California College of Arts and Crafts. Charles was elected a Fellow of the American Institute of Architects in 2007 in recognition of his contributions to design and architecture.

Greg Keffer

Greg Keffer brings to STUDIOS a diverse background and skill set crossing the broad disciplines of architecture, interiors, graphics, and branding. His ability to focus and extend a company's brand through simultaneous channels including design of spaces, messaging, and collateral, brings an integrated approach and valued service to his clients. Greg's agility and leadership as a designer strengthens his clients' brands, distinguishes them in the marketplace, and produces measurable results for their businesses.

Greg has demonstrated the firm's leading role as an innovator in sustainability, recently winning a national design competition for the Kingman Island Environmental Education Center, a platinum level LEED project located in Washington, DC. In addition he is working on similar projects for clients such as Bette Midler's New York Restoration Project. Both hospitality and mixed-use are a major focus for Greg. He continues to work with some of the leading brands on current projects including innovative hotel, restaurant, and retail projects around the world.

Greg received a Bachelor of Architecture and a Bachelor of Environmental Design from Ball State University. His projects have received recognition in numerous design publications including *Interior Design* Magazine, *Dwell*, *Contract*, *Architect* Magazine, *Boutique Design* Magazine, and *BOB International Magazine of Space Design*.

Tom Krizmanic
AIA, LEED®AP

Tom first came to STUDIOS' Washington, DC, office as an intern in 1988 and quickly became one of the most influential design leaders in the organization. In 1997, he moved to New York to lead the design efforts in what was then a fledgling office. Tom is currently the managing principal of the New York office.

Over the past decade, the New York office has achieved enormous success, due in part to Tom's dedication to strong, innovative design and his ability to forge positive, long-term relationships with his clients. Tom's

outstanding design talent and leadership skills have allowed him to be successful on a broad range of projects, including complex corporate offices, retail facilities, law firms, restaurants, and technology companies. His notable work includes projects for MTV Networks, Gucci Group, Linklaters, Nokia, and the New York headquarters for Bloomberg. Tom was also an integral team member for E*Trade Bank's Arlington headquarters and the speculative office/retail building at 610 Broadway in New York. His work has been featured in *Architectural Record*, *Metropolis*, and *Interior Design* magazines.

Tom earned a Bachelor of Architecture from Catholic University of America in 1990. He is a LEED-accredited professional, an active member of the AIA, IIDA, and Municipal Arts Society, and involved with the not-for-profit organization Publicolor as a painter and student mentor.

Jason deChambeau

Jason deChambeau joined STUDIOS' Washington, DC, office as an intern in 1993, and has since worked in the San Francisco, New York, and Paris offices. He was promoted to Principal in 2007, and continues to work in the Washington, DC, office.

Jason's work is primarily focused on commercial interior design. He believes in utilizing an intellectual approach to complex design problems, wherein projects are reduced to a logical series of smaller tasks, yielding efficient, appropriate, and award winning design solutions.

Recent notable projects include interiors and base building modifications for several law firms, as well as the headquarters for the International Brotherhood of Electrical Workers. Jason has worked with Venable, LLP and other law firms to relocate their offices into developments tailored to accommodate long-term occupancy. The IBEW headquarters project included the design of the organization's archival museum and, integrated within the architecture of the space, a solar trellis that generates enough electrical power to serve the executive suite. Jason also provides consulting services to developers to ensure that tenant occupancy issues are incorpo-

rated into their properties' designs. His involvement often affects the final massing of the building, transforming speculative commercial developments into build-to-suit environments.

Jason earned a Bachelor of Science in Interior Design from Ohio University in 1993 and is NCIDQ certified.

Christopher Mitchell
AIA

Chris came to STUDIOS in 1996. In 1999, he was instrumental in the creation of the Los Angeles office, where he is currently managing principal.

Under Chris' direction, the work of the Los Angeles office has fostered a broad base in both architecture and interior design, and has been successful in developing a diverse project list spanning high-tech, corporate, law, entertainment, educational, and retail/branding projects.

Chris' design philosophy focuses on the collaboration and dialogue between architecture and interiors within a framework unique to the West Coast—light, texture, and the natural environment. His work locally, nationally, and internationally focuses on the expression of clean, well-articulated experiential spaces with a modern vibe.

Initially, Chris' work with STUDIOS focused on high-tech and financial projects abroad in Tel Aviv and Shanghai. His most recent experience includes a diverse clientele with projects such as Microsoft Technology Centers in Irvine, New York, Atlanta, and Chicago; the headquarters of car research and information company Edmunds.com; the De la Guerra Dining Commons renovation and School of Engineering addition at the University of California, Santa Barbara; interiors projects for the Industrial and Commercial Bank of China in Shanghai; various projects for Disney, Warner Bros., and Cartoon Network; and interiors and branding projects for Sergio Rossi, Stella McCartney, and Nicole Miller.

Chris earned a Bachelor of Environmental Design from Miami University (Oxford, OH) in 1988,

and a Master of Architecture from the University of Pennsylvania in 1991.

Pierre Pastellas
DPLG

Pierre joined STUDIOS in 1991, and in the following year founded the Paris office, where he remains a principal today.

With more than 25 years of experience in architecture and construction management, he has extensive knowledge of local and European building codes and construction conditions, and has continuously contributed to STUDIOS' recognition in the European architectural community. His practice includes architecture and interiors in Western Europe, as well as in the Middle East and Asia.

Pierre's past projects include the Hemisphere office park in Versailles; the headquarters for La Redoute in Roubaix; the Genoa, Italy campus of Marconi Communications; and a variety of work for significant clients such as Bloomberg, Bouygues Immobilier, Vinci Immobilier, and Renault.

Pierre studied at the École Spéciale des Travaux Publics in Paris, where he received his Engineering Diploma in 1971. He received his Architecture Diploma in 1977 from the Ecole Nationale Supérieure des Beaux Arts, Paris.

Darryl T. Roberson
FAIA

Darryl is a founding principal of STUDIOS. He works out of the San Francisco office.

With more than 45 years of practice, Darryl has received national recognition and an extensive history of awards, as well as professional and community acknowledgment. As a founding principal, he has been instrumental in guiding the policies and the extraordinary growth and reputation of STUDIOS, nationally and internationally, as well as the design of major projects. He has been at the forefront of corporate architecture for his entire career, first in the establishment of interiors work as a legitimate and vital form of architecture, and more recently, in the design of urban development and institutional buildings. Darryl led the movement to create more flexible office environments, employing new systems and concepts to develop models for the physical organization and design expression of workplaces. His experience has encompassed innovative interiors for Fortune 500 and high technology companies, as well as law, financial services, and consulting firms.

Darryl has led such notable projects as the four-block Foundry Square office development in San Francisco, and the interiors for Petronas' headquarters in their landmark Twin Towers in Kuala Lumpur. He is currently serving as STUDIOS' principal in charge of the renovation of California Memorial Stadium and the new Student-Athlete Training Center at the University of California, Berkeley.

Darryl earned his Bachelor of Architecture from the University of California, Berkeley in 1960, cum laude. He was elected a Fellow of the American Institute of Architects in 1976, in recognition of his design work and contributions to the profession.

David Sabalvaro
AIA, LEED® AP

David joined STUDIOS in its first year of business and was promoted to principal in 1990. He works out of the San Francisco office.

During his more than 25 years of experience directing the design and management of large corporate, commercial office, and educational building projects, David has developed a pragmatic approach to design that seeks out aesthetic opportunities within limited budgets. He is a strong advocate for simple, elegant design solutions to a client's complex and technologically challenging program requirements. David's talent in the design and delivery of fast track and technically complex, large-scale projects has earned him regional and national recognition for design excellence by the American Institute of Architects.

David recently worked with the University of California, Berkeley on

the renovations of Le Conte Hall— which included research labs, offices, and a new center for theorists— and Cory Hall, home to the university's Electrical Engineering and Computer Science Departments. His past notable work includes signature projects and campuses for Apple Computer, SGI (Silicon Graphics), and Excite@Home, as well as the new Math and Computer Science Building for California State University, Bakersfield.

David received his Bachelor of Art in Architecture from the University of California, Berkeley in 1979.

Erik Sueberkrop
FAIA

Erik is a founding principal of STUDIOS and the Chairman of the Board. He works out of San Francisco, and regularly collaborates on projects with all offices.

As the principal designer for many prominent STUDIOS projects, Erik spearheaded the formation of the firm's philosophy, in which the natural history and cultural influences of a site are joined with the building program to give the project both emotional and intellectual resonance. His work is characterized by its emphasis on community and the dynamics of human interaction. Erik is active in planning, architecture, and interiors projects internationally. He has received numerous national and international awards for his work and is published frequently.

Erik's signature work for high technology clients—such as Apple, Silicon Graphics, and 3Com— helped establish worldwide workplace models to structure new and existing companies' social organizations and invest corporate architecture with greater meaning. His current work with higher education campuses has focused on developing quality of life spaces as a part of the basic program for office and research environments.

Recently, Erik has led such projects as a new office building for Catellus Corporation, and Stone and Youngberg's new corporate headquarters within San Francisco's historic Ferry Building. He is currently working on the Health Science Complex expansion at the

University of Cincinnati, as well as on several biotech buildings for Alexandria Real Estate Equities, Inc., and projects for the University of California at Berkeley, San Francisco, Davis, and Los Angeles.

Erik earned his Bachelor of Architecture at the University of Cincinnati, where he graduated magna cum laude in 1972. He was made a Fellow of the American Institute of Architects in 1994 for his contributions to design and architecture.

Brian Tolman
AIA, LEED® AP

Brian joined STUDIOS in 1997 and was instrumental in the growth of the New York office, founded in the same year. Guided by a sense of curiosity and an affinity for problem solving, Brian leads clients and colleagues in rich collaborations that produce dynamic, unexpected solutions informed by the program, site and culture of the client.

Building on his early experiences with many of STUDIOS' high tech clients, Brian has effectively guided a wide cross section of organizations through difficult technological, regulatory and logistical hurdles by reducing complex problems into simple, digestible components that can be systematically approached and resolved. Embracing technology in both design and process, Brian has streamlined project communication and output. This concept allows for more effective and efficient project delivery, developing projects that showcase new technological solutions that enhance the human experience.

Brian's knowledge and passion for technology integration in architecture has lead to the success of many recent and notable projects, including the award winning global headquarters for Bloomberg LP in New York, as well as the Interior Architecture for the IAC headquarters, a Frank Gehry-designed signature building. In addition, Brian currently leads ongoing design efforts for Liquidnet and the post 9/11 headquarters for the Port Authority of NY & NJ. Brian's work has been featured in numerous publications, such as *Metropolis, Architectural*

Record, Fast Company and *Business Week*. Brian earned a Bachelor of Architecture from the University of Cincinnati, is a member of the AIA and a LEED® Accredited Professional.

Thomas K. Yee
AIA

Tom came to STUDIOS' San Francisco office in 1987, and became a principal in 1990. He is the president of the firm-wide executive committee as well as the principal in charge of firm-wide marketing.

Throughout his 30 years as an architect, Tom has demonstrated superior capabilities in the design and management of large-scale, complex projects, and the coordination of sizable design and consultant teams. An outstanding designer, he also has a proven track record of producing exceptional results within strict budgetary and schedule constraints. His design work revitalizes traditional architectural forms, drawing inspiration from alternative shapes and materials, as well as light and structure. His experience encompasses corporate, civic, and university projects, along with a substantial portfolio of headquarters and regional offices for leading California law firms.

Tom's recent work includes the renovation and expansion of the De la Guerra Dining Commons at the University of California, Santa Barbara, the design of National Semiconductor's new corporate headquarters, and interiors for law firm Orrick Herrington & Sutcliffe's new San Francisco office, which was awarded a San Francisco AIA Award of Excellence.

Other notable projects include the master plan and design of BEA Systems' corporate headquarters, full-scope interiors work for Heller Ehrman White & McAuliffe in San Francisco, Menlo Park and Los Angeles, and interior architecture for the 1,800-seat Shanghai Grand Theatre in the People's Republic of China.

Tom received a Bachelor of Arts in Architecture, cum laude, from the University of California, Berkeley, in 1973. He received a Master of Architecture from the University of Michigan in 1976.

Michel Lallemand • Donny Lam • Joseph A. Landry • Patricia Lane • Lars Langberg • Jennifer Langford • Jennifer Laong • Sheerapan Laosillapacharoen • Timothy J. Larkin • Freddy Laun • Susan E. Lausten • Juliet Lavia • Melissa C. Lawton • Simon Lea • Christina Lee • Grant Lee • Hye R. Lee • Jane Lee • Jason Lee • Kim Lee • Mildred Lee • Ming Lee • Robert J. Lee • Suh-Yung Lee • Robert E. Lee III • Tessa Lefeubvre • Rita Lehimdjian • Serena Lei • Geoffrey Leibovitz • Christopher Leitch • Ines Lejarraga • Céline Lemercier • Timothy Lentini • Scott Lentz • Patricia C. Leon • Thomas G. Leon • R. Bruce Leonard • Robert J. Leonhardt • Pedro Lepori • Sylvie Leroy • Monica Leung • Heather Levine-Chesler • Lawrence Levy • Stanley Lew • Aquila Lewis • Gregory Lewis • Marlo Lewis • Steven Lewis • Shannon Li • Yuen Yung Li • Michelle Lieggi • Yu-Cheng Lien • Casey Lim • Lee A. Lindahl • Peter Lipson • Louise Little • Kevin Lloyd • Kenneth Locascio • Michael Logue • Chris Lohan • Steve Long • Marla Longshore • Ginnie Lopez • Monica Lopez • Michelle Lopez-Orsini • Gregoy Losson • Josiane Lourenco • Sally P. Lovett • Martha Lovette • Monica Lucas • Brooke Luckock • Alexis Luhrs • Peter Lui • Daniel A. Luis • Phillip S. Luo • Susan Lynch • Katie Lytle • Henry Ma • Werner Maassen • Heather MacDonald • Iain MacDonald • Stuart MacDonald • Alan B. Macewen • Sara Madgwick • Maricela Maese • Laurent Mahaut • Alexandra Mahinka • Ali Mahjouri • Jean-Luc Maignan • Keisuke Makiminato • Sonja L. Malbaff • Juan Mancheno • Kim E. Manning • Margaret J. Manning • Gregory Mantz • Lall Manwinder • Audra Manzand • Kenneth G. Marcus • Pat Marinaro • Christopher Markel • Elizabeth Marley • Charles Marr • Gladys Marr • Brandon Marshall • Chris Marta • Christophe Marta • Andra Martens • Elizabeth Martin • Isaiah Martin • Lynn Martin • Michael Masson • Anna K. Matko • Vincent Maury • Kimberly Mayrhofer • Jason McCarthy • Michelle McCarthy • Rhonda McClure • Elisha McCullough • Brian McDaniel • Kathryn McGlone • Michael McGlynn • Craig McHenry • Jonathan McIntyre • Darren McMurtrie • Joseph J. McNamara • Robin P. McNamara • Gail Meaker-Joseph • Daniel R. Meis • Marcia Melin • Frank Mendoza • Suzanne Mercury • Fre'de'rique Meyer • James Meyer • Ryan Meyer • Tony Michaels • Ben Mickus • John Milander Ii • Mark Milina • Tiffoni Milkowski • Ann Miller • Brian Miller • Carolina Miller • Courtney Miller • Gina M. Miller • Harley Miller • Jennifer Miller • Mason Miller • Justin Mills • Nathan Minch • Julie Minkunas • Ryan Misner • Christopher Mitchell • Sandra Mitchell • Elena Mitschkowez • Norma Mitto • Elaina Mixon • John Mixon • Darcy Mobraaten • Abby S. Moffat • Karim Mokdad • Marc Molina • Justin Molloy • Fabienne Mommaels • Alexis Monson • Manuel Morales • Charlotte Morel d'Arleux • David Moretz • Hidekazu Moritani • Pual Morrison • Laura Mosca • Kamala L. Mostert • Anne Mouradian • Amir Mousawi • Emmanuel Moussinet • Mary Muir • John Mulcahy • Lisa Munoz • Bryan Murdock • Margaret Murray • Teresa Lynne Murray • Katrina Musson • David Must • Irene Nafpliotis • Tetsu Nagata • Rachel Najafi • Frédéric Nakache • Noha Nakib • Gail Napell • Robert Nashed • Bryan Natinsky • Brian Nee • Bertrand Neel • Robert Nehrebecky • Melissa Newby • Ronald Ngiam • Barry Nielsen • Nancy Nienberg • Joyce Nilo • Gerald Nilsen • Fred Niner • Galia Nitzan • Ana Nolan • Rebecca Christina Noren • Brett Norton • Farnaz Nourmohammadi • Teresa Nowicki • James David O'Brien • Leo J. O'Brien • Michael O'Callahan • Joseph R. O'Connell • Thomas O'reilly • Elizabeth O'Brian • Femi Odubanjo • Tana Ogeden-Gee • David Ogorzalek • Jason Oringer Ojeda • G. Christina Old • Douglas Oleson • Ewa Olizar • Phillip Olson • Pasak Ongwattanagul • Ian Orlins • Joe Ortega • Jacek K. Ostoya • Connie Overman • Susannah Overton • Julia Ovesenni • Maria Isabel Pacheco • Piotr Paciorek • Miguel Padilla • Stefano Paiocchi • Mark Palermo • Andrea Panico • Koula Papanastasia • Jamie Paquette • Ben Parco • Manon Paré • Lauri K. Parkinson • Gilles Pasquier • Pierre Pastellas • Matthew Pateman • Jennifer Patterson • Claire Paulat • Carter Cobb Paxton • Craig Payne • Siohith Perera • Shirley Perez • Kara Perkins • Claire Perraudin • Cliff Peterson • Heidi Peterson • Kathleen M. Petzke • Deborah Pfeiffer • Marc Pfenninger • Julienne C. Piankoff • Pier Pierandrei • Justin Piercy • Brian Pilot • Tom Pinkowski • Nadine Pinto • Kasia Piotrowska • Ben Piper • David Piper • Remy Pires • Paul Pires da Fonte • Ste'phane Pitiot • Stéphane Pitiot • Cynthia Pitt • Amy Pokawatana • David Pol • Nicholas M. Polito • Jeannie Pope • Sean Porter • Jesse Portz • Sabine Pouget • Thierry Pourchet • Joanne Powell • Vijaya Pradhan • Taina Primaux • Emmanuel Prunevieille • Thomas Prusinski • David Pugh • Jill Pugh • Richard Pulley • Shelley Pyne-Hanley • James M. Quanttrone • Andrea Quenga • Alfred Quezada • Tomas Quijada • Pablo Quintana • Brian Quirk • Linda Race • Gene Rae • Salim Rafik • Aaron Ragan • Benjamin Ragle • Daniel Ramirez • Wesley Ramirez • Jason H. Ramos • Nageshwar N. Rao • Meredith